Asher the Thresher Shark

T0268825

Asher the thresher shark is very shy. Will it stop him from being a hero?

This picture book targets the /sh/ sound and is part of *Speech Bubbles 2*, a series of picture books that target specific speech sounds within the story.

The series can be used for children receiving speech therapy, for children who have a speech sound delay/disorder, or simply as an activity for children's speech sound development and/or phonological awareness. They are ideal for use by parents, teachers or caregivers.

Bright pictures and a fun story create an engaging activity perfect for sound awareness.

Picture books are sold individually, or in a pack. There are currently two packs available – *Speech Bubbles 1* and *Speech Bubbles 2*. Please see further titles in the series for stories targeting other speech sounds.

Melissa Palmer is a Speech Language Therapist. She worked for the Ministry of Education, Special Education in New Zealand from 2008 to 2013, with children aged primarily between 2 and 8 years of age. She also completed a diploma in children's writing in 2009, studying under author Janice Marriott, through the New Zealand Business Institute. Melissa has a passion for articulation and phonology, as well as writing and art, and has combined these two loves to create *Speech Bubbles*.

What's in the pack?

User Guide

Vinnie the Dove

Rick's Carrot

Harry the Hopper

Have You Ever Met a Yeti?

Zack the Buzzy Bee

Asher the Thresher Shark

Catch That Chicken!

Will the Wolf

Magic Licking Lollipops

Jasper the Badger

Platypus and Fly

The Dragon Drawing War

Asher the Thresher Shark

Targeting the /sh/ Sound

Melissa Palmer

Routledge
Taylor & Francis Group

LONDON AND NEW YORK

First published 2021
by Routledge
2 Park Square, Milton Park, Abingdon, Oxon OX14 4RN

and by Routledge
52 Vanderbilt Avenue, New York, NY 10017

Routledge is an imprint of the Taylor & Francis Group, an informa business

British Library Cataloguing-in-Publication Data
A catalogue record for this book is available from the British Library

Library of Congress Cataloging-in-Publication Data
A catalog record has been requested for this book

ISBN: 978-1-138-59784-6 (set)
ISBN: 978-0-367-64866-4 (pbk)
ISBN: 978-1-003-12668-3 (ebk)

Typeset in Calibri
by Newgen Publishing UK

Asher the Thresher Shark

Asher was a thresher shark

Who would hide away from fish.

Other sharks found it puzzling –

Fish was their favourite dish!

The **sh**arks would try to **sh**are with A**sh**er,

And just couldn't understand why

A**sh**er the thre**sh**er would pu**sh** the fi**sh** away –

He was really rather **sh**y.

Asher the **sh**y thre**sh**er **sh**ark

Had no friends in all the o**c**ean.

Any time fi**sh** or **sh**ark came near

He **sh**ot off, away from the commo**t**ion.

But A**sh**er had a secret

That no other **sh**arks knew.

He loved to spla**sh** in and out

Of the o**c**ean – like dolphins do.

A**sh**er's tail was long and **sh**arp,

Different to any other **sh**ark.

Underneath his colouring is quite light,

And on top it's rather dark.

A**sh**er's **sh**immering **sh**arp tail is why

He can spla**sh**, dive and leap,

Shooting out of the o**c**ean in full flight

Then da**sh**ing down, diving deep.

One warm day with sun **sh**ining,

A**sh**er saw dolphins leaping out of the o**c**ean,

Spla**sh**ing and pu**sh**ing past each other,

Oh boy! What a commo**t**ion!

A**sh**er desperately wanted to spla**sh** and play,

And **sh**are in all the fun,

But he was a **sh**y thre**sh**er **sh**ark,

And didn't know how it could be done.

Just then A**sh**er saw a dolphin get stuck

In a floating pile of tra**sh**,

A dirty **sh**oe, a holey **sh**irt.

He panicked and tried to da**sh**!

The dolphin couldn't escape and A**sh**er knew

He had to do something to save him.

He had to pu**sh** down his **sh**yness, be brave!

Sma**sh** through the rubbi**sh** and grab him!

So A**sh**er **sh**ot himself through the rubbi**sh**,

-sh-sh-sh-sh-sh-sh-sh-sh-sh-sh-sh-sh-sh-sh-sh-sh-sh-

And caught the dolphin on the way.

He pushed him through to safety –

While fi**sh** watched, **sh**outing hurray!

"You saved me!" gushed the dolphin

When the din had died away.

"How can I repay you?" said the dolphin.

"Well," A**sh**er said **sh**yly, "could I maybe come and play?"

So that's how A**sh**er the thre**sh**er **sh**ark

Came to be spla**sh**ing in and out of the o**c**ean,

Overcoming his **sh**yness, making new friends,

Playing and causing a commo**t**ion!